Formula for a Miracle

Formula for a Miracle

Look for Needs+Pray+Wait, Ready to Work

Tom & Ginger Blackburn

Copyright © 2005 by Tom & Ginger Blackburn.

Library of Congress Number: 2005901024
ISBN :   Softcover   1-4134-8615-0

All rights reserved. No part of this book may be reproduced or transmitted in any form or by any means, electronic or mechanical, including photocopying, recording, or by any information storage and retrieval system, without permission in writing from the copyright owner.

This book was printed in the United States of America.

To order additional copies of this book, contact:
Xlibris Corporation
1-888-795-4274
www.Xlibris.com
Orders@Xlibris.com

27810

Contents

Foreword 7

EARLY BEGINNINGS

Chapter 1: A Work Is Born 11
Chapter 2: Seeking Support 13
Chapter 3: The Beginning 14
Chapter 4: The Executive Board 16
Chapter 5: An Artesian Well 19
Chapter 6: The Early Meetings 21
Chapter 7: Help from the Community 23
Chapter 8: Willing Hearts 26
Chapter 9: The Well-Baby Clinic 28
Chapter 10: Monthly Clothes Auction 30
Chapter 11: The Summer Recreation Program 31
Chapter 12: Christmas at the Center 33

THE TRANSITION

Chapter 13: New Leaders Trained 37
Chapter 14: The Search for a Pastor 38
Chapter 15: God's Call to Tom Blackburn 39
Chapter 16: You're Hired for Twenty Years 41
Chapter 17: The Installation of a New Pastor 43
Chapter 18: Additions and Improvements 45
Chapter 19: Handing Over the Torch 47

BUILDING A NEW CHURCH

Chapter 20: Prayer for a New Church Building 53
Chapter 21: The Rough Road of Construction 55
Chapter 22: Miracles along the Way 57

FIRST FRUITS OF THE LABOR

Chapter 23: Help from the Congregation 65
Chapter 24: A Decade of Growth 67
Chapter 25: Changed Lives 69
Chapter 26: Changes in the Seventies 72
Chapter 27: The New Faces of the Executive Board 75
Chapter 28: The Dream of a Christian School 79

THE HARVEST CONTINUES

Chapter 29: The Birth of a Christian School 83
Chapter 30: The Lord's Supply 86
Chapter 31: A Time of Testing 88
Chapter 32: Revival of a Dream 91
Chapter 33: Celebration 93
Chapter 34: The Women Who Supported the Ministry 95
Chapter 35: But God 97

Foreword

The story that you will read is a true account of how God uses very human men and women to do a work directed and orchestrated by the divine Holy Spirit. The story began in the mind of God but was manifested on earth in 1947 and continues today, in the year 2004. The methods of the ministry have changed over the years, but the purpose remains the same. It is to look for needs; to pray about them; and to wait, ready to work, so that Jesus Christ will touch and change lives and fulfill his purposes on earth.

It was our privilege to be a part of this miraculous work during the years of 1960-1999. It is our desire that this account will be a faith builder and an encouragement to its readers.

EARLY BEGINNINGS

Chapter 1

A Work Is Born

And now these three remain: faith, hope, and love. But the greatest of these is love.

—1 Cor. 13:13

It took a lot of love for a sixty-five-year-old retired lady minister to come to a teeming tent city that boasted only river water for drinking and a main street inhabited primarily by gambling casinos and bars. But love was what motivated that little lady. It was a love inspired by Jesus, the King of love Himself.

Mrs. Leisher's acquaintance with what was to become Garden City began with a bus ride. She had come to Boise as a city missionary for the Northern Baptists from Colfax, Washington, where she had pastored a church. Her husband, Ralph, also a pastor, had passed away.

Ready to face a new challenge and following the Lord's leading, she came to serve Boise. Or so she thought. The impact of that fateful bus ride was to change the whole direction of her ministry. Her heart of love went out to the needs she saw before her. Here was a whole village of people in a place not equipped to meet their needs. Most of the dwellings were makeshift shanties. Some were tents. There were hardly any plumbing facilities and no central water system. Grocery stores were few, yards were almost nonexistent, and there was no place for children to play.

Poverty prevailed. There was not a church, a clinic, a school, or a library within two miles. Of the nearly six hundred children, 279 were infants or preschoolers, and 337 were of grade-school age. Their fathers were engaged in building Highway 20.

It was in March 1947 that a dream was born in Mrs. Leisher's heart. She aspired to begin a church in the midst of those people and to minister to their needs. Her mind was in a whirl as she thought of all the potential. It would be a place for children to play and for creative things to be done in a Christian atmosphere. It would be a place to come for social activities, for a hot shower, and for good drinking water. It would be a place where clothing could be acquired, and if the need arose, food would be provided. The possibilities seemed endless. It would take a miracle, but she wasn't worried. Her God specialized in miracles.

Mrs. Leisher developed a plan. She would work as if it all depended on her and pray as if it all depended on God. The miracle had begun.

Chapter 2

Seeking Support

Her first plan was to enlist the help of the Idaho Baptists in beginning a mission work on Highway 20. The plan met with resistance. Mrs. Leisher had been assigned as a Boise City missionary by the Idaho Baptist Convention. Her assignment did not include the project on Highway 20. There was no guarantee that the mission work would ever become a self-supporting church. The Idaho Baptists did not have the finances available to support a long-term work such as that would be.

"We will continue to pay your salary," they told her, "but we cannot support the kind of work you are describing."

Mrs. Leisher pondered, "I'll just have to come up with another plan. I'll go to the Boise Ministerial Association. Maybe they will have some ideas." That was what she did.

"I want the best, most dedicated men you can give me from your churches," she told them. "I need men who have a desire to help the needy and who can obtain the means to support this type of work. I also will need the backing of your churches—whatever you can spare a month to get us started."

The pastors from the Boise Ministerial Association were interested in helping with the work, and five of them gave her some names with which to begin.

After some time in prayer, she began to develop a plan. It was an ecumenical masterpiece. Five major denominations cooperated with the mission project that was to change the lives of many in the community that was to become Garden City.

Chapter 3

The Beginning

Five trustees and an executive board of ten members were chosen from the cooperating churches to attend to the business affairs of the project. They were to be a covering for Mrs. Leisher. There were five member churches in the organization: the Methodist Church, the Christian Church, the Congregational Church, the Presbyterian Church, and the Episcopal Church. The Idaho Baptist Convention was to pay her small salary.

She requested of the member churches their strongest Christian men to serve on her board of directors. In 1950, the list of these men read as follows: Homer S. Deal, chairman; John D. Gordon, secretary; John Studer; Walter Musgrave; E. E. Kidder; Gilbert G. Stamm; Elmer F. McIntire; Melvin E. Day; Robert Bruce Dunn; T. F. Meyer; and H. B. Schofield.

These men were asked to meet in the tearoom of the Mode Department Store in downtown Boise. At this meeting, Mrs. Leisher told of a Christian Center in the heart of the Highway 20 project. She described the needs of the area and the importance of a Christian outreach.

"When did this Christian Center get started?" The men questioned.

Mrs. Leisher's firm reply was "Just now. It began just now with you, gentlemen, as the first board of directors."

One of the first miracles to take place was the agreement and cooperation of all of the board members when they accepted her challenge.

In subsequent meetings, as each need arose, the men passed the hat, and the Lord moved hearts to meet those needs. The board purchased a lot on the west side of Forty-second Street, north of Federal Aid Route No. 20, and about one and a quarter miles from Fairview Junction.

> Pioneering in the rocky ground explored by the first supporters of the Community Christian Center brought the founders face to face with as

many, though different, obstacles as the early settlers in the raw West. Resources were meager. Physical properties were not easily obtained. There were barracks buildings available for purchase at Gowen Field, a World War II airbase, but funds for their moving were inadequate. Advocates of the Center were met with the argument that the need would fade away as Garden City developed a sound, acceptable community structure or that existing organizations in the Boise area would meet the problem by sharing the load in their several ways.(Dick d'Easum, Community Christian Center brochure, 1965)

God had other ideas. Determined prayer overcame the barriers. Dependence on God was the key. Mrs. Leisher knew that He was the One who had placed the desire in her heart to begin with. Once the work was started, He blessed the prayer efforts. Soon the center became a recognized successful force for good and an object of community pride.

Originally, two buildings had been purchased. One was used as the administration building. It was sixty-seven feet by twenty-five feet, and it afforded residential quarters for the director. In addition to a living-room area, two bedrooms, a bathroom, a library, and a heating plant, the administration building had a large kitchen equipped with an electric range and a large five-door refrigerator that covered one whole wall. The second building served as the assembly building. There was room at one end to have a kitchen and dining room. The middle area would serve as the assembly room for Sunday-school and worship services. The opposite end had two bathrooms with showers.

One day, while Mrs. Leisher was on her way to town, she had the urgent feeling that she should turn around and head for home. She returned just in time to see a large barracks building being moved on to the property.

"Where shall we put 'er?" she was asked.

"Put it here," she responded, pointing to the property line.

The men set the structure down right on the inside of the property line, and Mrs. Leisher promptly dubbed it "the third building." The name stuck. She never received any information as to who had purchased the building or donated it to the Christian Center. She put it to good use as a craft building. Later, as the congregation grew, the building was divided into three classrooms and a storage room. Each room was heated by a small potbellied stove.

Wholesome activities every day of the week drew the participation of young and old. The mission work began to take shape as it was nurtured by God's miraculous hand.

Chapter 4

The Executive Board

The men who comprised the executive board labored long and tirelessly on behalf of the Community Christian Center. They were individuals who were dedicated to the Lord. Once they made a commitment to the executive board, they took to their duties with enthusiasm. It was obvious to them that this work was of God. New members, invited to serve on the board, were men of influence, who knew how to get things done.

Frank Chalfant, an attorney, helped draft the articles of incorporation for the Community Christian Center. He was the legal "watchdog" for the center. Taylor Robertson knew how to raise the funds for much-needed projects. These men of vision were able to forecast what could be accomplished in this ministry.

The enthusiasm and vision of these dedicated men can be sensed in these lines penned by Taylor Robertson to prospective contributors in 1952:

> Like a miracle, through the sincere prayers, faith, and efforts of the Trustees and Officers of this Center, as agents of the sponsor, the Boise Ministerial Association, this ill favored Highway 20 area now has a very active youth-rehabilitation plant unique in Idaho, and even in the Northwest.
>
> The acute problem is the remaining capital debt of about $3,000, which is past due, as final installments to the house-moving contractors, plumbing and heating contractors, artesian well drillers, etc. (About three-fourths of the Center's plant improvements, including labor, have been donated by Boise service clubs and organizations, Boise churches, Boise businesses, and Boise individuals who were busy, but not too busy to spend their "gardening" time out on Highway 20, making the

Center what it is today.) To meet these "one-time" capital obligations, the Center's officers determined to place the problem of retiring the remaining capital debt in the hands of some thirty child-welfare-minded Boise individuals with the expectation that they might willingly erase, once and forever, the past-due debt, thereby making possible the strong continuance of this Center for years to come, the only hope of many a luckless child whose home happens to be "way out on Highway 20."

For my part as a member of the Board at this time, I selected yourself from this list of individuals who can help us out, and I want to take the time to call upon you in person before the 18th of September, to present the whole picture of the Highway 20 Community Christian Center, with which I have been working wholeheartedly since its inception, feeling confident that you will be glad to participate in abolishing the only remaining debt against this very real and very worthwhile institution.

We of the Board are certain this Highway 20 Community Christian Center is the finest interdenominational activity Boiseans ever might take a part in, and five hundred Highway 20 kids will forever be in your debt. (letter by Taylor Robertson to the contributors of the Christian Center)

During one of the first early executive-board meetings, the vision and whole purpose for the existence of the Community Christian Center were recounted. It was to be an interdenominational activity, originating for the purpose of empowering people of the community spiritually, mentally, physically, and socially.

The board members deliberated about how the articles of incorporation would be drawn up. They wanted the participation of many denominations but felt that because Mrs. Leisher was an American Baptist and the Idaho Baptist Convention paid her salary—and because American Baptist churches in the area were contributing greatly to food supplies, used clothing, and special needs—the property, in the event of dissolution, should go to the Idaho Baptist Convention.

The membership of the people who were to be served need not be American Baptist or even required to attend services at the center. Whenever a need arose, the Christian Center was to be available to help. The board members came from several denominational churches in Boise. Monetary gifts and help in various forms were gratefully received from many sources.

Mrs. Leisher acknowledged that the work of the Community Christian Center was the Lord's work and was to be carried out in His way. If she saw those who were sick or in prison, she would minister to them because as she did it "unto the least of these, she did it unto Him." The Christian Center was an outreach to the community. That was its origin and its purpose.

Mel Day, one of the board members, related the following story:

> One evening Mrs. Leisher summoned Mel. She was emptying out her cupboard as she filled a box for a poor family.
>
> "I want you to take this box to a family who is in need," she directed him.
>
> "But you should have that food yourself," Mel protested. "Besides," he continued, looking down at the name on the slip of paper she had handed him, "This fellow gambles away his money. He ought to be buying his own food!"
>
> Mrs. Leisher frowned at Mel and quietly spoke, "Mel, I'm not doing it for him. He has a family who needs the food. I'm doing this for the Lord." Mel, feeling duly chastised, delivered the box.

The Lord blessed her work. The Sunday school reported an attendance of one hundred and fifty. Children and adults were accepting the Lord as their personal Savior. The people in the surrounding area were having physical and spiritual needs met.

The Lord was moving in individuals, churches, clubs, and business firms to provide support for the work. Mrs. Leisher's undaunted faith was contagious. As the Lord's blessings were showered upon her, she faithfully gave Him the glory. The result was changed lives even for "the least of these."

Chapter 5

An Artesian Well

There was no central water supply in the early days of the center's existence for the community that was to be known as Garden City. The board decided a well was clearly needed and encouraged Mrs. Leisher to call a man to drill a well for the water supply.

After the driller had gone down sixty feet, he came to Mrs. Leisher, stating, "We have water now."

"Is it artesian?" she questioned.

"No, but it's good water."

"I have my heart set on artesian. Keep drilling."

The man continued to drill deeper. At 120 feet down, he came to her again.

"We've hit water," he explained.

"Is it artesian?"

"It's good water."

"I want artesian. Keep digging. I haven't the money in hand to pay you today, so you might as well dig deeper."

After the driller hit a dry hole, he continued down to 365 feet deep.

"We have water, and I'm not going any deeper, "the driller announced, emphasizing the last five words.

"Is it artesian? I want an artesian well."

"I don't know. But I'm not going any deeper." The driller began to pull up his equipment.

Mrs. Leisher walked over to peer down at the new well.

Glug, glug, glug. The water bubbled up in the hole. A broad smile curved Mrs. Leisher's lips. The Lord had given her heart's desire: an artesian well! That well supplied water to the people of Garden City for many months until the city provided a water supply.

Within a week, the bill for the drilling company was paid for by a member of Mrs. Leisher's former congregation in Wisconsin. That individual had sent the exact amount needed, with the following explanation: "I don't know what you need it for, but the Lord said to send this amount." The Heavenly Father continued to supply the needs of the center.

Chapter 6

The Early Meetings

After the barracks buildings had been acquired, Mrs. Leisher planned for a Sunday school. The word went out to all the families in the area that there would be classes in the barracks building on Forty-second Street. Two classes were formed in the beginning.

The older children and teenagers were taught by Mel Day, a young man who had been sent by Sam Skaag, of Whitehead Drugstore, to help with the work at the Christian center. Mel was from the First Baptist Church.

Mrs. Leisher directed him, "You take the older ones, and I'll take the younger ones because some of them are still in diapers."

Mel went about his work with zest, and soon he had a large group of children and teenagers.

In a short time, Mrs. Leisher drafted others to help with the classes. A young war bride from Wales, Edna Siggelkow, an Episcopalian, taught the primary classes. Jay and Martha Amyx, Southern Baptists, helped with the classes. A young couple, Gerald and Marilyn Irvan, new Christians, volunteered to help. They worked with the teens.

A theological conflict about what to teach never took place. The presentation of the Gospel was the main thrust of the lessons.

In a short time, the Sunday school had grown. The classes were comprised of children, with a few adults. Mrs. Leisher began inviting the women of the community to attend an adult class taught by Mr. Evans, who came from out of town. Special worship services were held in the large assembly hall on Easter and Christmas.

In August 1948, Mrs. Leisher began meeting with the women of the community. Seven women were at the first meeting, including Mrs. Leisher. She started the meeting with a Bible verse and a poem.

The state home-economics director offered to give the women instruction in sewing or cooking. Their classes were held on a separate day from the regular meeting. Mrs. Scarf of the State Family Life Department conducted sewing classes on the second and fourth Thursdays of each month.

Chapter 7

Help from the Community

Although abundant help was needed from churches and members of surrounding communities, the people who would benefit most from the Community Christian Center showed an eagerness to help as well.

The children themselves lent a hand to build the Community Christian Center playground. They showed ingenuity in improvising and built their own baseball backstop. They built rough but sturdy tables from cinder blocks and pieces of plank for the meeting room. The boys built steps for the entrances to the buildings.

Even though the children helped build the playground, Mrs. Leisher realized that the adult citizens would benefit from the ministry as well.

"A wholesome recreational Christian outlet for their energies will keep these children away from crime, and we do believe the people of Boise will realize the importance this place had," Mrs. Leisher spoke with conviction as she addressed various church and civic groups. Her words had a prophetic ring.

Soon after, the barracks buildings were in place, weeds were removed, a well was drilled, and sections of buildings were joined together. Several outstanding donations were received. One of these was a large five-door refrigerator obtained through war surplus and public donations. Folding chairs were borrowed from the school district during the summer months but had to be returned in September. The Chaussee-Swan Gravel Company leveled and surfaced the baseball field. A jukebox was found at the country club and donated to the Christian Center. Boise Kiwanis Club provided chocolate milk for an occasional party at the center. Later, they furnished milk daily for the summer recreation program. Other donations of food and materials were received along with volunteer labor.

Wallboard was donated for the volunteers to put up on the main building. Later, a coal-burning furnace was installed to heat the main room, which became the sanctuary. The other building was used as a parsonage and an office for the director.

The Christian-center board wanted to develop a well-balanced recreation program and facilities for the children. Mrs. Leisher requested that tools be donated for the boys' workshop. Other needs were filled from unused items stored in attics and garages. A piano, a bookcase, small tables, a baby bed, an electric stove, and two sewing machines were donated.

The women who attended the monthly meetings began to pay the fuel bill with earnings from the bazaar and special fund-raisers in 1949. Plans were made to put a kitchen in the auditorium building. A man by the name of Mr. Lee did the work. The women painted the kitchen and the hall. After the kitchen was completed and the dining room was fixed up, the women decided to make some rules for the use of the facility. Whoever used it was to leave it in good condition or forfeit the right to use it. Later, a small fee was charged to those who used the building.

In September 1949, the women held a potluck and invited their husbands to come and build shelves in the furnace room for food storage. A Fall Festival was held to stock the shelves with fruits and vegetables. Twenty-nine quarts of fruit and ten cans of vegetables were received.

Inmates from Idaho State Penitentiary constructed a slide, a jungle gym, swings, and a teeter-totter. Sand was brought in for a children's sandbox. One of the inmates, James Arard, who formerly taught art at Bacone College, painted an oil portrait of Jesus praying in the Garden of Gethsemane and donated it to the Christian Center in December 1948. It hung in the sanctuary at first and was later moved to the parsonage when the director became concerned that the chairs for the choir would damage it. Twenty-five years later, it hung over the baptistry in the new building and remained there for the next thirty years.

The denominational churches—such as the Methodist and Congregational, the First Baptist, the First Methodist, the First Presbyterian, and the Lutheran churches—all led hobby nights held at the Christian Center from 1951 to 1953. The Union Thanksgiving Service gave their fall offering to the center in 1952.

Individuals contributed toward the expenses of fuel for the coal furnace that heated the main hall and the administration building.

The men of the community agreed to build a stage. The women purchased glass dishes for the kitchen, and in March 1949, they began to clean the auditorium weekly for Sunday services, using the money from some of the fund-raisers to help with the fuel bill.

Individuals helped with numerous repairs over the years. The storage building was reroofed. Contractor Jay Amyx set the administration building on a firmer foundation. Insulation was put in the ceiling.

Fairview Acres Lateral Water users held meetings in the main hall in exchange for the center's water usage.

Over a period of time, the program at the center thrived under Mrs. Leisher's able leadership and the generous contributions of its many supporters.

Homer S. Deal, then president of the executive board of the Community Christian Center during the years 1949-1950, included the following paragraphs in some of his letters:

> In less than two years the Center has become an integral part of this community, ministering to those in need and giving a Christian training to a large group who otherwise would go without help or assistance of a Christian nature.
>
> The operating expense of the Center has been underwritten by member churches of the Boise Ministerial Association, and the solicitation for additional funds from interested parties will be applied to furnishing the necessary work to complete the Center. With the finished installation, the community should then have many years without further additions, meeting the needs of this fast growing community, who up to this date have been unable financially to care for their needs along this line.

Chapter 8

Willing Hearts

How did the Garden City people who benefited from the efforts of the community respond? They enthusiastically threw themselves into the work. When Mrs. Leisher suggested having a fall bazaar to raise funds for necessary purchases, they readily agreed.

The first fall bazaar was held in November 1948. It was to become an annual event for many years. It was planned as a fund-raiser to provide for curtains in the auditorium and to buy songbooks for the Sunday school.

"First, we'll have a small community sing," Mrs. Leisher planned. "And we'll have a tea table. You, ladies, will bake and bring two dozen cookies each."

"Will that bring in enough money?" one of the ladies questioned.

"We'll have more than that to sell," Mrs. Leisher explained. "If any of you do fancywork, you should bring that to sell also."

"Will anything be planned for the children?"

"Of course, we can't forget them. We'll plan a fishpond. We will have lots of little things, like crackerjack toys. We need things that are still good, but you don't use anymore. We'll have balloons, small toys, and the like. Of course, we'll have to decorate a screen. All the prizes will be hidden behind the screen. The children will have to 'fish' for them with real fishing poles. Someone will stand behind the screen and tie the prizes to the line."

"That sounds like so much fun!" the women responded with enthusiasm.

"The youth group will sell candy," Mrs. Leisher added.

The bazaar turned out to be a huge success. The fishpond was the major attraction, with a double line until everything was gone.

Larger articles were auctioned off, with Mr. Carl Burt, of First Baptist Church, auctioning every item—even his necktie!

The earnings were $103.80—a big reward for the women's efforts.

Just as the women had readily agreed to a fall bazaar, they willingly followed Mrs. Leisher's lead in other matters as well. Her demeanor exuded authority. The people wanted to comply with her wishes. An example of this was when the need arose for a choir director.

One Sunday morning, Barney Siggelkow brought his Welsh war bride, Edna, to the church service. Mrs. Leisher greeted her, and during the conversation, she asked, "Do you sing?"

When Edna nodded, Mrs. Leisher beamed. "We need a solo for this morning," she stated with authority.

Edna recalls that she hadn't planned to sing a solo, but she could not refuse the white-haired little lady.

Mrs. Leisher, pleased with Edna's voice, assigned her the role of choir director. The two women became good friends, and as the years followed, Edna was a valuable help to the Christian Center. She became the president of the newly formed Women's Society. She often helped Mrs. Leisher with her housework and drove her around after her car had been dismantled, one piece at a time, by the local pranksters.

Edna became a faithful member of the Community Christian Center and a dedicated Christian. She continued in her role as choir director for over forty years, taught Sunday-school classes for all ages, and was a source of inspiration and wisdom.

One of the significant outreaches Edna had while she was at the Christian Center was the music group called Melody Makers. They were a quartet that traveled to nursing homes, Boise Rescue Mission, and various churches with their music. They always brought a Gospel message wherever they went.

Why was Edna's contribution so significant? Because she had learned from her teacher Mrs. Leisher to see the need, to pray, and then to wait, ready to work. The miracle continued as Edna willingly followed Mrs. Leisher's lead.

Chapter 9

The Well-Baby Clinic

During the monthly women's meeting, a nurse, Ms. Simontou, from the health center in Boise, gave a talk on immunization. Following this first meeting, she came for one hour a week, on a school day, to examine children who had been ill and to approve their return to school. It was during this time that Mrs. Leisher birthed the idea of a well-baby clinic. Most of the young mothers had no transportation or means of obtaining monthly checkups for their babies.

As Mrs. Leisher talked to community groups about this need, a young pediatrician, Dr. Loy T. Swinehart, offered his services at the Christian Center on a monthly basis. There would be no charge to those who brought their infants and young children. He offered medical examinations and made sure immunizations were available. He checked as many as twelve babies each month.

Volunteers manned the clinic: visiting with the mothers, weighing the babies, giving PKU checks, and writing it all down on a chart for the doctor.

People were referred to the clinic on a need basis. A nurse from the Department of Health and Welfare visited with the mothers about diet, what to expect in stages of development, etc. A volunteer made the new appointments as the mothers were leaving. The nurse sent out notices of appointments each month.

Preparations had to be made in advance for the monthly clinic. A volunteer swept the floors; placed the chairs for the mothers; and prepared the kitchen for an examination room with an examination table, a wastebasket, tongue depressors, padding, and paper for the examination table. She set aside an area for inoculations, separated from the waiting room by a screen.

Dr. Swinehart asked nothing in return for his service. The only thing he received, besides the gratitude of the community, was a bump on the head. An old kitchen window in the dining room had a foldup door. The examination table was just under the window. One day the foldup door dropped down and hit the doctor on the head, knocking him unconscious.

Another humorous incident occurred when a father brought his eight youngsters in for immunizations. The little boys waited nervously in line for the "big injection." During the immunization of the fourth child, the nurse inquired of the father about his own immunizations.

"How long since your last immunization?" she asked.

"Oh, I don't need any," the father hastily replied. "I've never had any, and I don't intend to start now!"

"Oh yes, you do," the nurse shot back. "We'll do you last."

The father left suddenly and was not to be found when his turn came. He was outside, hiding in the car.

Chapter 10

Monthly Clothes Auction

Mrs. Leisher often told the following story of how the monthly clothes auction began. There was no school in Garden City; and the children were bussed to Whittier, Franklin, and Mountain View elementary schools. Some children had no clothing fit to wear for school attendance.

One day she saw a young boy sitting dejectedly on the steps of a building. It was the middle of the morning, and Mrs. Leisher knew he should have been in school.

"Young man, why aren't you in school?" she questioned.

"You wouldn't go to school either if you had to wear your mother's shoes!" he retorted.

"Indeed, I wouldn't," Mrs. Leisher sympathized.

This was the beginning of the monthly thrift store. Used clothing was solicited from churches, individuals, and service groups. The women sorted it and repaired it when necessary. Each month, free-clothes days occurred. Boxes of clothing were put out for people to go through and take what was needed. It wasn't long before Mrs. Leisher realized that the needy people were grabbing up clothing and sorting it later to see if they had the right sizes to meet their needs.

"What these people need is not charity," she thought, "but a bargain." She began auctioning off the clothing for a nickel or a dime. The money was used to care for the needs of the Christian Center. If someone was unable to pay even that small price, they were to come to her privately, and the clothing would be given to them. The clothes auction eventually evolved into a thrift store, open several days a week, as space became available.

Chapter 11

The Summer Recreation Program

After the playground had been set up, children began appearing on the property daily. They had enjoyed the hobby nights and the Sunday-school classes, but especially during the summer, they needed some supervision as they played on the playground.

Mrs. Leisher attempted to get a recreation director from Boise City Recreation for five days a week throughout the summer. One of the first directors was Ona Beth Sigman. She lived in the community, and her children attended the center's programs.

The first regularly scheduled program was in the summer of 1952. The program consisted of daily prayer, table and outdoor games, a story hour, a playhouse for kindergarten children, and arts and crafts for the older children. For two weeks during the summer, daily swimming lessons were offered. The children were bussed to the pool at Lowell Elementary School. Every Friday, there was a free swim at the pool. In addition to play on the playground, movies were shown once a week. There was softball for the boys and men. The Kiwanis Club furnished free milk to the children. That summer, ten boys went to YMCA camp on paid scholarships.

Another popular event was the Shrine Circus. The El Korah Shriners provided buses to take the Garden City children to the circus. The recreation director, Sunday-school teachers, and parents all pitched in to help with the children. Sometimes as many as three hundred children were loaded onto buses early in the morning for circus day. They were taken to the Meridian Speedway, where the circus was held. The children oohed and aahed at the clowns and elephants, the high-wire acts, and the animal stunts; but the concessions attracted the most attention. By the end of the circus, the sunburned, tired children were loaded back on the bus by the equally sunburned, exhausted adults. The children had enjoyed a fabulous day at no expense to themselves, thanks to the kindness of the Shriners, and they would live on the memories of that day until the next year when the ritual was repeated.

The whole summer recreation program was rounded out by two weeks of intensive Daily Vacation Bible School.

That first year there was programming for fifty-two days and an average of 293 hours. The total attendance for the summer was 2,664.

Recreation was such a success that it was held each summer for at least thirty years. One of the longest-term recreation directors was Vera Morrow, who will long be remembered for her loving, faithful service.

Chapter 12

Christmas at the Center

Another of the successful programs at the Christian Center that benefited the children of the community was at Christmastime. Churches, organizations, and individuals all contributed to make Christmas at the Community Christian Center a memorable event. The Baptist churches in the area filled Christmas quotas each year, consisting of a gift for a boy or a girl, clothing for a boy or a girl, a gift for a teen, and gifts for men and women. Schools and civic organizations collected canned goods and staples to be given in food boxes. Some organizations sponsored individual families that had specific needs. The Shriners collected gifts for children to be given at the Christmas program. The Christian Center congregation supplied sacks of candy, and the Sunday-school teachers prepared special Christmas programs to be presented by their classes. The night of the program, the building was filled with an unusually large number of eager children and adults, aflutter with excitement. Carols were sung; children nervously clustered on the platform to give their performances. At the close of the program, "Santa" strode in with a large bundle of presents and offered one to each child there.

A few days before Christmas, the pastor and congregational leaders took the food and gift boxes to the homes of those in need. Miraculously, there always was the right amount of food and presents. While sometimes there were a few items left over, there was never a lack.

One evening, after the gifts and boxes had been delivered, there were two food boxes and one gift box left over. Inside one of the boxes was an envelope that had some extra cash. On Christmas morning, the phone rang. There was a family in need. Could the director go see about it?

When she arrived at the trailer house, the director found a man sitting on the steps with his head in his hands. The door behind him was open. The man looked up at her and shrugged. There was no need to close the door. The power had been shut off. The house was cold. In the living room, two teenagers and a woman huddled together for warmth. When the boxes were carried in and set on the table, the woman began to cry.

"Thought you could use these," the director explained. "Look! Gifts for teenagers and for each of you!" Holding up the envelope, she said, "I have enough money here to get your power turned back on. I'll take care of it for you."

After returning to the center, it was the director's turn to cry. The Lord hadn't made any mistakes. He knew all along who would need those boxes on Christmas day and how much money was needed to have the power restored.

THE TRANSITION

Chapter 13

New Leaders Trained

After Mrs. Leisher began having monthly meetings with the women, they encouraged their husbands to come to church.

The clothes auction also drew the interest of the adults in the community. One lady, Millie Williams, declined coming to church because she had nothing to wear. Her friend Betty told her about the clothes auction. Millie went and, in her own words, "found the prettiest blue dress." She began to come to church and brought her children.

One day she persuaded her husband, Clayton, to come with the family. Jay Amyx was preaching when Clayton's heart was touched, and he surrendered his life to Jesus.

Gradually, as the adults began coming, Mrs. Leisher trained them to be leaders in the church. By the time the Blackburns arrived at the Christian Center in 1960, its leaders were Clayton and Millie Williams, Carl and Ruth Grothaus, Jerry and Marilyn Irvan, Jim and Agnes Moore, Grant and Lucy Young, and Barney and Edna Siggelkow. They formed a strong nucleus for later church growth.

The men helped with tasks that needed to be done on the church barracks building, such as painting, helping install the coal furnace, and putting wainscoting in the main church building. These men later spent hours building the new church structure.

The women took on leadership responsibilities as they grew in the Lord. They became Bible-study leaders, Sunday-school teachers, and youth leaders. Some served as choir members, one as a pianist, and one as a nurse in the clinic.

Chapter 14

The Search for a Pastor

Mrs. Leisher served faithfully at the Community Christian Center for over ten years. She had masterminded the development of a growing missionary work, with the Lord's inspiration and blessing and the help of countless individuals and churches.

By this time, she was past her midseventies and had enlisted the help of lay pastor Jay Amyx to preach on Sundays. Rev. Orville Stiles had preached revival services. The program now had not only Sunday-school classes that met weekly for all ages, but it also had worship services.

Parents, interested in what their children were so involved in, began to attend the services. One parent related the following:

> When Carol came home and reported that one of the boys pulled her pigtails repeatedly, I decided to go and find out who he was. It turned out to be a son of the man who was preaching, but the sermon was so good that I just stayed. After that, I began going regularly.

Mrs. Leisher saw the need to find a young man who would not only preach but who would also learn from her and eventually take over all of the responsibility that she carried. She contacted an American Baptist seminary, Berkeley Baptist Divinity School, to send a candidate who was getting ready to graduate. That summer, the young man came. He loved working with the children. He was enthusiastic with the program possibilities. He had plenty of ideas he wanted to try, but as he put it, "No one can work with that woman."

At least two other young men from the Idaho churches came to work with Mrs. Leisher, but she wanted none of them on a permanent basis.

"The Lord will send the right one when he sees fit," she insisted. She wasn't in a hurry. Jay Amyx was doing a good job, and she would bide her time.

Chapter 15

God's Call to Tom Blackburn

Tom Blackburn wasn't sure why he had ended up at Linfield College in McMinnville, Oregon. He had grown up on a dirt farm near Hotchkiss, Colorado. He was sixth of six children. He had almost no money in his pocket, but he desired to be a coach and to major in sociology. He had been a low-average student in high school, with a big interest in sports. His high-school principal hadn't encouraged him to go to the meeting for college-bound students. About the same time, a series of events occurred that indicated the Lord's hand on Tom's life.

A substitute music-band teacher, Mr. Caylor, encouraged him to write to Linfield College for an application. He did, and he was accepted.

A kind lady in Hotchkiss, Margaret Swisher, liked Tom and offered him a loan of $500 to help him get started.

By the end of the summer, young Blackburn stepped on a bus headed to McMinnville, Oregon. He took some campus jobs and got a job at a Shell service station to work his way through school. He knew and loved the Lord, but at that time, ministry was not his goal.

At the end of the first year, Tom did not intend to return to Linfield, but by the time school started in the fall, he again boarded the bus for Oregon, with another $500 from Mrs. Swisher in his pocket.

It was during Tom's second year at Linfield that Tom met Ginger Nelson, a young Christian who had dedicated her life to ministry.

They began to attend church and Christian activities together. As their love blossomed, they set a weekly prayer date to determine if the Lord wanted them to marry and serve him together. Both felt they were being led into Christian Center work.

One of the activities they mutually enjoyed was a ministry outreach to Eola Village, a migrant labor camp. One evening, Tom was there without

Ginger. It was pouring rain, and the children were all gathered into a large community building to play games. One small boy sidled up to Tom and smiled shyly.

"I brought you something," he said, looking up at Tom with a smile.

"Oh, what is it?" Tom asked, wondering what one poor little boy would bring him.

The child thrust his hand into his pocket, searching for something. After a bit, he drew out a grimy, wrinkled dill pickle and held it up triumphantly in his hand. Face shining, he blurted out, "I brought you this dill pickle!"

Tom's heart was deeply touched. He knew that the child and his family subsisted on a diet of beans and corn bread. A pickle was a rare treasure. This little one had saved his to share with his new friend.

This simple incident confirmed to Tom that he would serve those less fortunate for the rest of his life. He considered it his call to ministry.

Five years later, following seminary training, Dr. Harry Coulter, executive minister to Idaho, asked Tom and Ginger to candidate at the Community Christian Center.

Chapter 16

You're Hired for Twenty Years

The cold and blowing snow over Donner Pass had delayed the Blackburns several hours as they made their way from the seminary in Berkeley, California, to Boise, Idaho, to candidate at the Community Christian Center. They had planned to arrive at their destination in time for the executive-board meeting at noon. When they finally pulled in, it was well past three in the afternoon. The board members had gone home, leaving Mrs. Leisher to greet Tom; Ginger; and their small son, Tim. She graciously led them to her living quarters in the administration building.

The afternoon was spent getting acquainted and visiting. Mrs. Leisher explained the program of the Christian Center and how it had all begun. She detailed the role of the executive board; the "helps" program that was in place; the weekly meetings of the congregation, youth, and children; and how she felt the Lord had led her thus far. Tom was to preach in the morning service the next day.

The Blackburns and Mrs. Leisher "hit it off" immediately.

"Now you've been told," she began, "that no one can get along with me, but that's not true. You must treat me as a mother-in-law. Just listen to what I say and agree with everything I say, and then do as you please."

They all had a laugh over that. Then she continued, "I'm not opposed to change. I just don't want change for change's sake. If you have tried what is in place and you find something will work better, then you can think about changing the way we do things."

The following morning in the worship service, Mrs. Leisher introduced the Blackburns. After Tom's message, Mrs. Leisher, who had remained on the platform during the sermon, stood up and faced the congregation.

"How many of you want the Blackburns to come?" she queried.

The congregation responded with raised hands.

"That's fine," she stated. "We'll see you in two weeks, and you're hired for twenty years!"

Pastor Tom, as Mrs. Leisher had dubbed him, was flabbergasted. He hadn't expected a vote so soon. He hadn't even prayed about whether or not he wanted to accept the offer. In retrospect, he determined Mrs. Leisher and the Lord had decided for him.

Two weeks later, in January 1961, his on-the-job-training began. Mrs. Leisher had moved into a small cinder-block house on the Christian Center property, leaving the larger quarters in the administration building for Tom's family. Every morning, Tom took the morning paper to her and stayed for a short while as Mrs. Leisher versed him on the "how's and why's" of the ministry. She remained the director of the Christian Center while Tom was the pastor.

"I've been the director for thirteen years. It will be awhile before people start coming to you. Be patient, and in time, they will let you help them," she told him wisely.

Pastor Tom was a willing student, and he eagerly learned all she had to impart.

Chapter 17

The Installation of a New Pastor

On the first Sunday in February 1961, a new minister was officially welcomed to the Community Christian Center. The following is an excerpt from the February 9, 1961, issue of the weekly newspaper *Garden City Gazette*:

> Officials of the Center and the Baptist Church spoke at the installation service to express the joy of everyone of having the Rev. Thomas Blackburn and his family at the Center.
>
> Especially significant to us were the remarks of the Rev. Estle M. Leisher, who has served the Center so long and so well since the day it evolved from her dream to reality, and Mr. Jay Amyx, the layman who has "preached," guided, and worked for the Center over the years. These two spoke not as person losing a daughter, but rather as those gaining a son.
>
> And so the new pastor of the Community Christian Center received the official welcome of not only the Center, but of the Idaho Baptist Convention, and the Boise Ministerial Association. And he received the individual welcomes, in the form of a handshake, from many members and friends of the Center.

Thus, Pastor Tom began his first pastorate, one that was to extend over a period of thirty-nine years and one that was as much a blessing to him as it was to the Community Christian Center.

Pastor Tom with the children on the playground.

Chapter 18

Additions and Improvements

Shortly after his arrival, Pastor Tom organized five Little League base teams. The boys practiced regularly on the Christian Center grounds, but sli into bases was hazardous because of the prolific puncture vine that grew on ball field. The ground was very rocky and weedy, and it boasted no irriga system.

Pastor Tom urged the executive board to look into putting a lawn sprinkling system in back of the center. Many hands worked together to comp the work.

The project was the result of numerous people and groups working toget Morrison-Knudsen Company brought in twelve truckloads of topsoil at the req of Truman Joiner, an executive-board member.

The men of the Christian Center congregation installed a sprinkler syste pull water from the nearby irrigation ditch.

Pastor Tom contacted a youth group in San Lorenzo, California, to come spend a week picking up rock, raking the topsoil smooth, and planting seed.

Taylor Robertson, a board member, donated the seed, and Harold Fi also a board member, donated thirteen ash and linden trees to plant for sh The Boise Kiwanis Club set them in the ground.

Boise Cascade, along with board-member George Bachellor, donated seve five cubic yards of soil aid.

Within a few weeks, a beautiful carpet of green grass had replaced rocky, weed-covered area the boys had used as a ball field. The project testimony of what could be done when many groups work together to accomp a desired result.

An additional improvement took place with the addition of a library to Ga City. In 1960, the bookmobile from Ada County Library began rolling thro

rden City. One of its bimonthly stops was in front of the Community Christian
nter on East Forty-second Street. The response of the children in the area was
nendous. During the hour and a half of each stop, Mrs. Gladys Skinner
ped with book selections, and an average of a book a minute was processed.
oughout the period—from May 24, 1960, to January 1961—the children
d a total of 1,298 books and adults read 152, according to the coordinator of
 bookmobile Mrs. Rachel Fenske.

This enthusiasm for reading led to the beginning of the Garden City Library.
oom in the Sunday-school building was set up as a library. Books were donated
n individuals and from service organizations. Outdated books from school
aries found their way to the first Garden City Library.

Gladys Cole, a member of the Community Christian Center, processed the
ks and became the first librarian.

After the new city hall was built in 1978, the library was moved from the
ristian Center to its new quarters in city hall.

As the congregation began to grow in the little barracks-building church in
rden City, plans began to form in Mrs. Leisher's mind. Eventually, a new
rch would have to be built. The barracks buildings had been built at Gowen
ld to last for seven years. When the time came for them to be removed, the
ristian Center Board had been given permission to buy the buildings. Those
racks served the Community Christian Center's congregation for an additional
teen years.

In 1963, Pastor Tom Blackburn and Mrs. Leisher went for a drive. They
ped on Ustick Road at the Ustick Elementary School, a structure that had
ntly been built. As they walked around the building, Mrs. Leisher observed
 the classrooms had been built around the gym and cafeteria.

"This would be a good plan for a church," she decided. "The classrooms
ld be built around the sanctuary."

The contractor of the school was contacted, and with a few adjustments, a
 was drafted for the new building. It would be at least four years before
thing was done in the way of construction, but the plans were in place.

Chapter 19

Handing Over the Torch

)r four years, it had been a regular ritual for Pastor Tom Blackburn to pick
: paper each morning and take it next door to Mrs. Leisher. Then for the
our and a half, she would visit with him about the center, the contacts to
de, the programs that were in place, the needs, and how to pray about
She told him how each program worked and why she had set it up the way
*d.
?emember, just treat me as you would your mother-in-law," she would say
twinkle in her eye. "Listen to everything I have to say. Agree with everything
and then do as you please!"
ie type of mentoring she gave Pastor Tom was the best apprenticeship he
have received. She methodically laid everything out and answered his
ons. That, with his on-the-job training, equipped him to be a faithful servant
Lord. "Work as if it all depended on you and pray as if it all depended on
eek out the needs and then try to meet them with the Lord's help."
ter four years, one morning she handed the books over to Pastor Tom.
you know everything I do," she explained. "It is all up to God and you."
ithin the month, she fell ill with the illness that took her life.

* * *

Mrs. Leisher Goes Home

s. Leisher went home to her Lord in October 1964. The community was
l at her passing, but they knew that she had trained the new pastor and
r well. They would miss her and would speak of her often over the years
lowed.

Her funeral service was held at the First Baptist Church in Boise, and was buried in St. John, Washington, beside her husband.

The following is an article from the *Idaho Statesman*, October 12, 19

> The Rev. Estle M. Leisher, 78, 212 E. 42nd Street, Garden City, a civic leader and organizer of the Community Christian Center, died early Sunday at a Boise Nursing Home.
>
> Mrs. Leisher was born August 21, 1886, at Pinconning, Mich., and took her early schooling in Michigan, attending Racine High School and a high school in Milwaukee, Wisconsin. She attended normal school at Whitewater, Wis., and was married to Ralph W. Leisher while at Whitewater, in 1903. Their wedding trip was to Cincinnati, Ohio, where both attended and were graduated from Cincinnati Bible Seminary. After a time in evangelism, both were ordained in 1923, to the Baptist ministry at Lapeer, Mich.
>
> Mrs. Leisher served pastorates at Almont and Mason, Mich., from 1924 to 1934. The couple served at Colfax, Wash., from 1934 to 1942, and at St. John, Wash., from 1942 to 1945. Mr. Leisher died at St. John in 1944, and Mrs. Leisher came to Boise in 1946.
>
> She organized the Garden City Community Christian Center in 1947, and served on the board of directors until 1960. Mrs. Leisher was honored for her civic endeavors by the Altrusa Club, which awarded her the "Pin of the Year" in 1952, and by the Boise Exchange Club, with its "Golden Deeds Award," in 1960.
>
> She is survived by three sons, L. Byron Leisher, Boise, president of Whitehead Drug Stores, Inc., the Rev. Dr. Ralph Leisher, Dowagiac, Mich., and Quentin R. Leisher, Chicago, Ill., vice-president of Kendall College, and seven grandchildren.
>
> Services will be conducted at 11 am, Tuesday, at the First Baptist Church, with the Rev. Thomas J. Blackburn, Community Christian Center, the Rev. Dr. Mack McCray, and the Rev. Harry Steger of the First Baptist Church, and the Rev. Dr. Frank L. Rearick and the Rev. Chester Northrup, of the First United Presbyterian Church officiating.
>
> Interment will follow at St. John, Wash., on Wednesday.

The late Rev. Estle Leisher, founder and director of the Center.

Mrs. Leisher, the founder and first director
of the Community Christian Center.

Following Mrs. Leisher's death, the congregation made a decision to purchase an organ as a memorial to her. A committee was formed consisting of Edna Siggelkow, choir director; Agnes Moore, pianist; Mel Day, deacon; and Pastor Tom Blackburn.

The committee gathered at Dunkley Music, on Capitol Boulevard, and saw many beautiful instruments. They discovered immediately that the $750 savings would not be adequate to purchase a suitable organ for the church. They looked at some very small new organs, and some very large used ones, but their focus returned to a medium-sized Hammond, with two keyboards and a full pedal. The price was $2,600. The committee decided to lay this decision before the Lord and the congregation.

For several weeks, different organs were brought to the Christian Center to try out. The decision was made to put the $750 down as the down payment on the Hammond organ.

Finally, a Sunday was set aside to celebrate Communion in memory of the Lord's sacrifice and to dedicate the entire offering in memory of Mrs. Leisher and her sacrifice for the Garden City people. The offering was taken, and Communion was celebrated with gratitude and praise. The bread of life was broken as the congregation shared the Word of God.

When the offering was counted and the organ dedicated, the amount needed had been supplied. There were checks from friends of Mrs. Leisher and checks to the church from all over the United States.

BUILDING A NEW CHURCH

Chapter 20

Prayer for a New Church Building

"When are we going to begin building our new church?"

The question came from one of the ladies of the Community Christian Center. For months, they had been talking of building a church structure. The barracks building was too small, and they had been holding two services each Sunday morning. Mrs. Leisher and Pastor Tom had discussed this possibility years before. The executive board debated it.

Some of the board were reluctant to "go out on a limb" with a new building.

"We don't even know what will be here twenty years from now," one of them argued. "It would be too risky to plan a new building here."

Some of the other board members were more farsighted. "Look what the Lord has done with this place. There is no limit to the lives that can be touched with a new facility."

The board and the church members prayed about it. A congregational meeting was held. Jay Amyx encouraged the building, but he cautioned the congregation to stand behind the pastor. They decided to initiate a building fund and save for it rather than go into debt.

When Edna Siggelkow raised the question about when they would build the new church, Pastor Tom responded, "Why don't we pray about that right now?"

As one, the group at the Bible study in the barracks parsonage knelt and began to pray for the Lord to direct and bless their efforts. Results of that prayer meeting began to manifest in the weeks that followed.

Pastor Tom contacted Red Amyx, a friend who was a building contractor. After looking at the plans and praying over them, Red suggested Tom to contact a building contractor who was a recent amputee. The contractor's name was Harold Ellis. He had been a building contractor in California, but after he had developed cancer and had to have his leg removed, he was no longer able to work.

Pastor Tom went to visit Harold, and after explaining his need, he asked Harold to come and help with the new church building.

"Well, you've come to the wrong man," Harold replied. "I'm not able to work for you."

Pastor Tom went home and prayed about the matter. The Lord impressed on him that he was to go to see Mr. Ellis again. Once more, he was refused, but the longer he prayed about it, the stronger came the impression that Harold was the man.

After the pastor's third visit, Harold became irritated. "What is the matter with you?" he demanded. "Are you blind? Can't you see I have a leg missing?"

"I don't want your leg," Pastor Tom persisted. "I need your mind. There's nothing wrong with your mind!"

Harold thought about that for a while, and then he accepted the assignment.

Chapter 21

The Rough Road of Construction

Early in 1965, Pastor Tom talked with the executive board about the need for a new building. Attendance that year had leapt from 118 on Sunday mornings to 155. Since two services were necessary, the congregation was planning and praying for a new church: the board agreed to look into it.

The congregation was challenged to raise $5,000 within a two-year time frame, and a businessman promised to match it. When the $5,000 had been raised, the businessman changed his mind. But the congregation was not discouraged. Demonstrating Mrs. Leisher's faith, they continued to work and to raise the money. By 1967, $12,000 was in the building fund.

Pastor Tom went to the American Baptist Extension Corporation (ABEC) to see about a loan for the new building. He received communication back that they could receive a loan after the paperwork was filled out. Over the next thirteen months, papers were filled out and sent, only to receive no response from ABEC. Pastor Tom called the organization every few weeks but only received excuses why the loan hadn't been issued.

At the regional convention in Seattle in 1968, he spoke with an individual from ABEC, who promised to get back to him in five days. After five weeks, the pastor called them. He still had received no loan. By this time, the congregation had broken ground and had begun building with the money they had in savings and the money that had come in on a daily basis for that purpose.

Finally, Rev. Robert J. Smith, executive minister for the Idaho Baptist Convention, wrote to ABEC, reminding them of their promises of a loan.

Meanwhile, Pastor Tom traveled to the churches in the regions of Idaho, Oregon, and Washington, telling them of the needs of the Community Christian Center and of the plans for the new building. Many of the Baptist churches were excited about the work and gave generously to help with the new facility.

Finally, on September 1, 1970, papers were drawn up by ABEC for a loan of $31,000 to build the new structure. Up to the time the loan was secured, money kept coming in for the building fund. When the loan was made available, the other monies stopped. As soon as the loan money was used up, funds again came in. The congregation took this as a sign of the Lord's blessing on the building but also as a lesson that they were to depend on the Lord, not on a loan, for their provision.

Chapter 22

Miracles along the Way

Some of the miracles that took place during the construction of the building were the changes that took place in the lives of the individuals involved. One example of this can be seen in a rough individual named Jake Wisdom. Jake was a man who wouldn't lay down his trowel. The Wisdoms didn't have much in the way of material goods. Jake wanted to give what he could. What he had was the ability and the desire to lay concrete flooring. At the time, Jake was not yet a Christian. He made a decision to follow Christ during the building project. This act of service was his donation, contributing to the decision to commit his life to the Lord Jesus.

Because he had severe arthritis in his hands, Jake had to begin his day early before the mixer arrived. He would curl his fingers around the handle of the trowel—rubbing them, opening, and closing them—until they formed to the handle, and he felt he would be able to smooth the concrete. Finally, he would give the signal, and as the concrete was readied, he began to smooth it. Hour after hour, he was on his knees, praying and working the cement.

Jake never mentioned the pain he experienced, but one had to only watch him work to evaluate the measure of his love and the pleasure he received from giving himself to help build the church building.

Another miracle was the creativity the Lord gave the bricklayers from Pullman Brick Company. They had been contracted to lay brick for the church building. The men had been working hard to complete the job. All of them had agreed to donate one day to labor without pay to help with the work.

The crew came early in the morning and began their work on the back of the sanctuary wall. Half of the team worked on one side and half on the other. They were to meet in the front of the sanctuary. All went well for a time, and then one of the workers realized he had a problem.

He spoke to the foreman, "It doesn't look like it's going to come out even when we meet at the front wall. Look! There are an uneven number of layers. How will we meet together in the middle of the wall?"

"You're right," the foreman agreed. "Stop the work! We need to have a conference."

They attempted to make up for the mistake by increasing the amount of mortar on one side so the bricks would line up with the other side. When this did not solve the dilemma, they prayed and deliberated among themselves about how to resolve the situation.

The Lord gave one of them an idea: why not insert a cross of contrasting white brick between the red walls to detract from the mistake? Why not make it look like that was part of the plan in the first place! This kind of creativity was of the Lord, who makes beauty out of unsightliness just as he makes something wonderful out of scarred lives.

That white cross was before the eyes of the congregation as they turned to leave the services each Sunday in the years that followed.

The unselfish and enthusiastic support of youth groups from Washington and Oregon—who, though knowing none of the individuals at the Community Christian Center or ever having seen the place, gave of themselves to raise money and to come and work on the new church building—was still another miracle. They saved the center countless hours and expense.

They donated time and labor to help not only with the construction efforts but also to help with the summer programs for the children. Two different groups came from Washington and scrubbed down the bricks after the walls were up. It was a long and tedious work. The young people lived in the old church-barracks structures for a week to ten days at a time. Their sponsors worked alongside them and prepared their meals.

In the mornings, the youth helped with Daily Vacation Bible School. Afternoons were spent scrubbing down the brick walls, cleaning up the construction site, and making themselves useful in many ways. In the evenings, they attended teen Bible school with the local youth. After a lesson each evening, the youth enjoyed a variety of fun times, such as a hayride, swimming, a watermelon feed, a backward-progressive dinner, and softball games.

On one occasion, a youth was heard to comment, "You mean I saved all my money to come here and work like this? Some vacation!"

Normally, there was very little grumbling. The kids did a wonderful job, and fast friendships were formed with the visiting youth and the local teens.

A youth group from Oregon raised enough money to purchase wooden folding doors to divide sections of the fellowship hall into classrooms. Pastor Tom had challenged them to raise the money, and they took the challenge eagerly, raising a total of $1,200.

When the building was nearly completed, another group of young people from Washington State came and helped install the pews in the sanctuary.

The commitment of these teens was an incredible testimony of faith in action. It was an inspiration to the members of the Community Christian Center and to the community itself.

Still, another miracle along the way was that of the roof for the building. The foundation had been laid. The floor was in. The bricklayers had done their job. The walls and trusses were completed, but no money had come in for the roof. Autumn had arrived, and soon the rains and bad weather would begin. As always, when there was a need, the congregation and its leaders went to work and prayed.

The pastor and his members had determined not to take out another loan, following the scriptural admonition to "owe no man anything but love." They had learned from past experience that the Lord would supply. For days, they worked and prayed, but the money was delayed.

One day, Pastor Tom received a call from an old friend of the Community Christian Center. "How is the building coming?" Mrs. Forney questioned.

"It is coming great. We only have one problem," Pastor Tom responded.

"What is it?" countered Mrs. Forney.

"It's our roof."

"What's wrong with it?"

"We don't have one," Pastor Tom answered.

"How much will it cost to put one on?"

The pastor gave an estimate.

"You get the bids, and I'll send the money," Mrs. Forney instructed.

Three bids were submitted. One was for $1,800, one was for $1,250, and the third was for $1,070.

Pastor Tom accepted the third bid. That afternoon, when he went to the mailbox, Mrs. Forney had sent a check for $1,000. The Lord had again supplied the need!

The roofing company went to work and completed the roof within a few days.

They finished about four o'clock one afternoon. Thirty minutes later, it began to rain, and it continued for three months. During this time, the finish work was completed. The Lord is never too late.

Pastor Tom in front of the sanctuary of the new church building.

The last thing built on the new sanctuary was a tower to house the church bell. The bell for the old church had come from the steam engine of a train that used to run between Boise and Idaho City: engine 2309. It had been donated to the Community Christian Center in the fifties.

The new church needed a larger bell. The old Linder School had closed, and at the time of its closing, the school board wanted the bell, but the owners of the building were reluctant to part with it. It was taken down from the building and stored in a school board member's barn. It remained there for a long time. Eventually, it was donated to the Community Christian Center to use on its building.

After the completion of the new church, Barney Siggelkow, a longtime member of the Christian Center and a former employee of Gate City Steel Company, volunteered to build a bell tower. He worked on his design, and he prayed a great deal over it. The day finally came for the tower to be placed on the church. Crane West came to set the bell tower on the building. Barney held his breath and prayed some more. Would it fit? The Lord had guided his hands. It was a perfect fit. The bell was mounted on the tower, and ever since, it has rung out proudly to announce church services, weddings, and the arrival of each New Year!

The outside of the church building, showing the bell tower.

FIRST FRUITS OF THE LABOR

Chapter 23

Help from the Congregation

The congregation was no longer willing to sit back and receive help from others.

As they grew in their commitment to the Lord, they also grew in their desire to contribute to the financial needs of the Community Christian Center. In addition to tithing, they also tried fund-raising. One of the fund-raisers that the congregation pursued during the completion of the church building was a waffle booth at the Idaho State Fair. They applied for a permit and a space on the concessions row. They received the permit and some passes for the workers to get into the fairgrounds. The first year, they only sold waffles. There were breakfast waffles and dessert strawberry waffles piled high with whipped cream. The profit was moderate, but the center had gained exposure. They decided to make it an annual event.

As time progressed, each year brought improvements to the waffle booth. It doubled, then tripled, in size. The menu expanded to include hamburgers, hot dogs, soft drinks, sausages, and bacon and eggs, in addition to the waffles. Each summer for several years, the congregation realized a progressive profit. Their booth gradually moved up to a more desirable spot on concessions row.

The workers chatted with the fair attendees and the carnival workers. They sang and capitalized on their opportunity to witness. One customer wanted to know "How you get into this club? It is a fun place!" The folks in the booth invited him to church; and he came, accepted the Lord, and stayed.

The crowning year was the one when the booth made over $9,000 profit. Over time, the fair board stopped issuing passes and began charging more for the spot on concessions row. It became increasingly difficult to make a profit. The congregation decided that they had "circled that mountain long enough." It was time to do something else, but all who had participated in the fair booth would fondly remember "the week of the waffle."

The interior of the sanctuary in the completed building.

Chapter 24

A Decade of Growth

Shortly after the dedication of the beautiful new sanctuary, the congregation of the Community Christian Center began to grow. New training programs were begun to help the congregation grow spiritually.

Evangelistic services, led by Rev. and Mrs. Sam Kliensasser, spurred the congregation to begin reaching out to friends and family and to bring them into the church.

Evangelistic outreach was taught, and training sessions were conducted. Discipleship classes were formed to welcome the new converts and to help them mature spiritually.

The congregation increasingly took on responsibilities, sat in on board meetings, and helped with fund-raising projects.

They planned, financed, and built a new parsonage for the pastor and his family. The impetus for this came from a family who, a decade earlier, had been hostile to the new pastor. Changed hearts had resulted in changed lives.

In 1976, Pastor Tom reported to the executive board eighty-six baptisms in a period of two years!

As the congregation thought of ways to reach out to the community, they realized the need for a free medical clinic. After much prayer and planning, several medical doctors in the Boise area agreed to come to the Christian Center on a weekly basis for a free medical clinic. One of the women in the congregation, Ruth Grothaus, a nurse, volunteered her time to help and to be responsible for the equipment in the clinic. A doctor from Nampa, Dr. McIntire, donated his time, and several of his collogues gave of themselves. Sample medications were prescribed, and if necessary, referrals were made.

The clinic was operational for two years until Ada County Health became involved and moved the clinic to Boise.

Head Start was organized and met in the building for a time, and senior citizens' lunches were served in the fellowship hall. The TOPS Club met there regularly for years.

The executive board questioned where the money was coming from to pay for the various projects, and Pastor Tom's only response was "From a lot of praying!"

Chapter 25

Changed Lives

Shortly after Pastor Tom and Ginger had come to the Community Christian Center, the pastor spoke at the YMCA. He mentioned the "cycle of poverty" that was in Garden City. Children of a poor family would drop out of school and try to find work. They would marry early and form the same type of family they had left school to escape.

One of the Garden City residents took exception to Pastor Tom's remarks that were printed in the local paper. She called him to her home and gave him to understand that not all the families in Garden City were like that.

"We are trying to build Garden City up, and you are tearing it down," Edna Adams scolded. "You are not welcome here, and furthermore, I will do all I can to get you out of Garden City!"

Pastor Tom left her home with a resolve to "love her into the Kingdom." He knew it wouldn't be an easy job. At Christmastime, the youth group went to her home to sing Christmas carols. On May Day, the pastor sent Edna Adams a bouquet of flowers. This went on for several years.

One day, her daughter's husband, Harvey, had an automobile accident. Edna told her daughter, Buelah, to call Pastor Tom. When a granddaughter wanted to get married, she was sent to see Pastor Tom. Gradually, the family learned of his love for them.

First, Harvey and Buelah; then Dee and Edna; and, eventually, twenty-two family members surrendered their lives to Christ and were baptized on Thanksgiving Day. They became members of the Community Christian Center.

One day, in the mid-1970s, Pastor Tom was again called to Edna Adam's house. He and Ginger sat in the same living room, with the same people, but this visit was quite unlike the first visit in 1960. With love in their hearts and on their faces, they told the Blackburns of their desire to build a parsonage for them.

They promised to help spearhead the project and to build it with their own hands. They kept their word. In 1976, Pastor Tom's family moved in to a beautiful new parsonage on East Forty-eight Street. It was completely paid for and lovingly built with the sweat, tears, and hard work of the congregation, spearheaded by one family. The Lord had worked a miracle of love in their hearts.

The Lord continued to change hearts. One of the men who allowed the Lord to change him was Don Brown. The story containing his testimony follows:

> "If there's anything I can't stand, it's religion!" Don Brown spoke adamantly. Don, a saddle maker by trade, was talking to Pastor Tom one day as the pastor entered the shop after a riding lesson with Don's wife, Jean.
>
> "Me too!" agreed Pastor Tom.
>
> "I guess you didn't hear me right," Don raised his voice and spoke again.
>
> "If there's anything I can't stand, it's religion!" Don tugged hard on the saddle he was lacing and looked defiantly at the pastor.
>
> "Me too!" the pastor repeated quietly.
>
> Don looked up, his eyes wide. Finally, he shook his head and spoke, "This isn't going at all like I expected."
>
> Pastor Tom explained the difference between religion and relationship, "Religion is man reaching up to God by a set of man-made rules. Relationship is God making a way for man to be made right with God by sending his son Jesus to live among men, to die in atonement for their sins, and to rise again to give man victory over sin and death."
>
> As they talked about it, Don began to come to an understanding of what Christianity was all about. Before long, he and all of his family accepted Jesus as their personal Savior and began attending the Community Christian Center. They brought more family members and many friends to the center so they too could accept Jesus.
>
> Don and his family formed a Blue Grass singing group called the String Band Review. They traveled around to churches and Western gatherings, bringing their music and a Gospel message.

Another man whose life was changed was Kenny Jones. Kenny was a gold miner from Yellow Pine, who came down to Garden City for repairs on his truck. He had a wife, two children, and a couple of golden retrievers.

One day, he came upon Pastor Tom outside the church building. They began visiting, and the conversation turned to spiritual things. After that, when he came to town, he always looked up Pastor Tom.

One evening, he came striding into the church office and told Pastor Tom he wanted to be baptized. When the pastor questioned him about his understanding of baptism, he affirmed that it meant he had a personal relationship with Jesus, and he wanted to make a public profession of his faith.

"I want to do it right now," Kenny insisted, "and I don't want anyone else around."

"But public means you need to do it in front of the people. We need people around, and it will take at least twenty-four hours to fill the baptistry."

"Nope," Kenny argued, "I don't want no baptistry. I want to do it outside, and I want to do it now. How about doing it in the river?"

"You need to do it in front of witnesses," Pastor Tom countered. "I will have a group of people here in about an hour for a meeting. They could be your witnesses, but it is early spring, and the river is too cold. How about the irrigation ditch? The water has started running in it now."

It was decided, and in a short time, about eight people gathered around the ditch to watch the baptism. People driving by thought someone was drowning since drowning had occurred in those ditches in the past. Before the baptism was over, about thirty-five people had watched Kenny profess his faith in Jesus Christ as his personal Savior.

Kenny came out of the water like a shot and was so grateful he paid Pastor Tom with a few little flecks of gold he had stored in a small pill bottle. The gold was from his mine in Yellow Pine.

Chapter 26

Changes in the Seventies

The ministry experienced modifications in the seventies. It took on a wider scope to fit the needs of the times. One of these changes was the addition of a soup kitchen.

The Lord brought about its establishment in a miraculous way. He placed a dream in the heart of a Catholic nun. Sister Stephanie and her friend had been praying for the Lord to feed the hungry in the Boise area. One day, as she was praying, the Lord impressed on Sister Stephanie that she should begin a soup kitchen for the hungry. "You feed them" were His exact words. She went to her parish priest, and she told him about her burden to start a soup kitchen.

"You have a great idea," replied the priest, "but you can't do it here."

She talked to other priests in several parishes, with the same response. Finally, she went to Father Peplinski.

"That is wonderful" was his response. Then he continued, "If you have a crazy idea like that, you should go down to Garden City and talk to Tom Blackburn."

Pastor Tom was in his office when Sister Stephanie appeared at his door. She told him about her burden and the responses of the priests she had contacted.

"That is a wonderful idea," Pastor Tom agreed. "When would you like to start? How about next week?"

Sister Stephanie was stunned. "You mean I can do it here? I couldn't possibly start for two weeks. Oh, that is wonderful!" She hugged Pastor Tom and danced around the room with him.

Within two weeks, the soup kitchen was up and running, with volunteers from several different churches. Food began coming in, and even though the program was not a line item on the Christian Center's budget, there was always enough food.

One day, soon after the program was started, Pastor Tom noticed a paper sign on the entryway door. It read, "We will feed the first twenty-five people who come to the soup kitchen." He pulled the note from the door and marched into the kitchen. The woman who was in charge of the soup kitchen for the day was the only one in the room.

"What is this?" Pastor Tom demanded.

"Why, it's a notice for the soup kitchen. We have enough food for twenty-five people, and that is all."

"What about the twenty-sixth person who may be hungry?"

"They won't be able to eat. We only have enough food for twenty-five."

"The Bible says, 'Feed the hungry.' It is not my problem if we don't have enough food. It is God's problem. You cannot put that sign up. We will feed as many as are hungry," Pastor Tom retorted.

The soup kitchen never turned anyone away and never ran out of food. The Lord is always faithful. The soup kitchen served as the hand of the Lord, ministering to those who were hungry and giving hope to the hopeless.

Carl was one such person. He wandered into the soup kitchen one evening, cold and hungry. He had tried many avenues to find peace and love, but they had eluded him. The soup kitchen was different. People were friendly, happy, and loving. The very atmosphere when he stepped into the building spoke of peace. Intrigued by the atmosphere, Carl began coming regularly. The food warmed his body; the love, his spirit. He decided to begin attending church.

It was in church one morning that Carl gave his heart to Jesus. His whole countenance changed. Before, he had had a lost, wild look. Now, the love of Jesus flooded his face and shone out of his eyes. He became a regular at church and brought others with him. His was a simple, powerful faith.

Carl was with the church body only a few years before he went home to his Savior. He left behind little wooden evidences of his love for Jesus as he fashioned clocks, bookends, toolboxes, and bookholders to be given away. Finally, he carved a shepherd's crook for Pastor Tom as a symbol that he was a shepherd to his flock.

The Lord's ministry through the soup kitchen brought a blessing to many lives. Carl's story is just one example of that blessing.

Danny was another example of a changed life. Lee Watson was in charge of the soup kitchen the evening Danny walked in. Lee, who had a heart for people, saw the weariness and discouragement written on Danny's face.

"I'm cold and hungry," Danny said. "Could I get something warm to eat?"

"Sure thing" was Lee's response as he heaped a plate high with good food for Danny. "Come on over and sit down," he invited, walking over to a table. When he set the plate of food down, Lee also took a seat himself. The men began to talk. Danny had no job, no place to live, and no family to speak of.

The next night, he was back. "Just thought I'd have another go at that good food," he spoke with a shy smile.

Danny kept coming back, and soon he began to show up during the day to help Lee with odd jobs around the Christian Center. Lee was always cordial, and he always found a job or an errand to occupy Danny.

Danny stayed around for several months. One day, Lee directed him to an ad for summer help at Yellowstone National Park. Danny answered the ad and secured the job. Lee didn't hear from him for several months. Then one day, he received a letter. The postmark was from Yellowstone Park. When Lee opened the envelope, a check fell out, along with the letter.

"Just wanted to let you know," the letter read, "while I was working here, I received word that I had inherited some money from my uncle's estate. I want you to use this money for the soup kitchen. When I came in that first night, I planned to eat a hot meal and go out and commit suicide. When I walked in, you gave me warm food for my body, but you also talked to me and gave me hope. You believed in me, and you gave me your friendship. You saved my life. Maybe you can do the same for someone else."

The check was for $1,000!

Chapter 27

The New Faces of the Executive Board

As the Christian Center congregation began to take more responsibility for the planning and programs, the executive-board members began to question whether or not the Christian Center remained a mission that the churches should support. The new building brought questions about whether it had become a church congregation much like those that had been lending their support.

The confusion prompted the then executive-board chairman Mel Day to write a letter to Rev. Robert Smith, the executive minister of the Idaho Baptist Convention. Copies of the letter were sent to the executive-board members and to Pastor Tom. In the letter, Mel explained how the Community Christian Center functioned in the early days and how it had been sponsored by the Idaho Baptists and the Boise Ministerial Association.

There follows an excerpt of the letter, explaining the transition into what the Christian Center had now become:

> At first ALL of the teachers, officers, workers, etc. came to the Community Christian Center from other church denominations. However, Mrs. Leisher immediately began to show and teach those who were being ministered unto, how they, with the Lord's help, could minister unto others. She organized a Women's Society, appointed deacons and deaconesses, trained Sunday school teachers, organized recreational play periods, conducted Vacation Bible School, established the Boy Scout troop, organized people to come in from the churches to conduct parties, wood work and leather work classes, the well-baby clinic . . . it would take pages and pages to describe the things she did to show the Lord's love and her love to everyone. Suffice to say, it was Mrs. Leisher's individual and personal efforts that made everything

and EVERYONE "go." These things she did as she went about her daily tasks, doing whatever was placed in front of her to do, with her complete and unshakeable faith in the Lord as she did His will to the best of her ability until the time of her death.

Initially all funds for the operation of the Community Christian Center came from the sponsoring churches and gifts and donations from many Christian persons, as individuals. Mrs. Leisher taught the people to bring their offering to the Lord, no matter how small it was. These offerings she used for the needs of the people. As time went on, she trained more of the folks from the congregation to help with the operation of the Community Christian Center. Through the years, the Community Christian Center has grown, developed, and changed, just as we have seen our children and grandchildren grow, develop and change. The folk of the congregation are doing more and more of the work and taking on more responsibility for its operation. Today the Center has grown to more of an actual church itself.

Change of itself, is not necessarily good or bad, but things do and have changed. Along with the congregation changing, the members of the Executive Board have also changed. Now that the new church building is built and practically paid for, and the parsonage has been completed and paid for, and the folk of the congregation are taking the responsibility for the operation of the Community Christian Center, the result is that the Executive Board members know less and less of the operation.

Things are not as they used to be, and from a practical point of view, can never go back to the way they used to be. We must all press on and go forward as we try to do the Lord's will as He reveals it to each of us.

Following the receipt of the above letter, congregational members were put on the executive board as full board members, and the transition to full responsibility began.

In 1977, the Idaho Baptist Convention launched a program to withdraw their support of the pastor's salary and set in motion a plan of withdrawal over the next five years, allowing the congregation to become increasingly responsible for paying his salary.

After the sanctuary was completed, the local churches began to withdraw their support. They no longer saw the Garden City Christian Center as a needy mission field but rather as a church that should support itself.

Community support, such as clothing and food being donated for use by the needy, continued to be strong. The First Association of the American Baptist

Churches in Idaho, along with local churches from the Boise Ministerial Association, continued to enthusiastically support the work as a mission field. Food, clothing, toys, etc., were readily given.

The predominant thinking was this is a struggling young work. They are growing as a congregation and are much like the other Christian churches in the area.

About this same time, in a monthly account to the executive board, Pastor Tom reported there had been five weddings, two baptisms, and one funeral; a representative from the congregation had spoken at the First Presbyterian Church of Boise that the Week of the Waffle, the congregation's fund-raising project at the Western Idaho Fair, had grossed a record-breaking $11,394.15; the radio program *Bible on the Table* was continuing each Sunday morning at seven forty-five on radio station KFXD; senior-citizen luncheons continued twice each week, along with delivering meals to shut-ins; the Council on Aging was trying to obtain funds to increase the meals to four or five times a week; the well-baby clinic continued to be held the third Thursday of each month, with thirty-one babies brought in for examination and vaccination; the Garden City Optimist Club sponsored an Explorer Scout Troup, which met weekly at the center; the assistance program continued as the congregation was able to help a fellow who was out of work and money. He had been disabled as much of his hip was destroyed while he was in the service, and the work he could perform was limited. They were able to pay his motel bill and then find him a job as a caretaker at a home where he was provided lodging in addition to a small salary. God was able to use the Community Christian Center while He led this man to the place He had picked out for him; the congregation had voted to absorb the utility expenses of the two old buildings and the parsonage.

Yes, God was changing and growing the ministry, but the mission was the same: being available for Him to work His purpose out through the Community Christian Center.

The Transition to the Christian Center Board

In 1977, plans were made to change the direction of authority from the original executive board to a board made up of members of the Community Christian Center. More congregational members were added during the seventies. Many of them were not from Garden City. Tithing had increased, and while the congregation was not yet fully self-supporting, they were paying many of the bills.

A finance board had been established, and a treasurer was to be elected from that board to take over the financial responsibilities that had been held by Pastor Tom and Phyllis Waller, his secretary. The finance board would also be responsible to take over responsibilities formerly held by the old executive board.

For a time, the old executive-board members remained on the board to help the new members in the transition.

The congregational members valued the wisdom, faith, belief, advice, and dedication of the members of the old board, who had served so long. They requested that they remain on the executive board and serve in an advisory capacity after the transition.

For several more years, six of these committed men—Truman Joiner, Frank Chalfant, Harold Finch, Claude Marcus, Elmer McIntire, and George Pullman—continued to be on the executive board.

The Community Christian Center had become more of a church than of a mission. The ministry still reached out to the poor and underprivileged. Local people and congregations still contributed to the work, but now it was more voluntary than obligatory.

Chapter 28

The Dream of a Christian School

After the church building had been completed in 1971, the congregation had considered having a school in the new facility. The classrooms around the sanctuary were large, and there was no reason not to use them during the week.

The board and the congregation had decided to begin with a day-care center since that seemed to be the greatest need at the time. The school-aged children were bussed to Whittier, Franklin, and Mountain View elementary schools. Junior-high youngsters were bussed to Hillside Junior High, and high school-aged children were bussed to Capital High School after 1960. However, in the 1970s, there were no schools or day-care centers available for Garden City children.

A preschool was begun, with Ginger Blackburn as director and Marsha Grothaus as teacher. The mothers who were receiving public assistance to pay for day care while they trained for potential jobs were the largest group of patrons.

The preschool flourished for a year and a half before the lack of funds forced its closure. Although the preschool was gone, the dream of a school remained. It seemed that the Lord wouldn't have the beautiful new facility sit idle during the week and only be in use on Sundays. This seemed like a poor use of space.

Several years after the preschool closed, the pastor was approached about the possibility of using some of the space during the week for a Head Start program. This was a government curriculum designed to prepare children for placement and success in the government schools. The Christian Center agreed to house the Head Start until a more suitable location could be found.

After two years, the Head Start officials told Pastor Tom the religious pictures would have to be removed. Instead of agreeing to that, the pastor told Head Start they would have to relocate.

It would be another eleven years before the dream of a Christian school was realized. When it happened, it was the Lord's timing and done in his own way

THE HARVEST CONTINUES

Chapter 29

The Birth of a Christian School

One of the congregational members came to Pastor Tom one day in 1983. She knew that Pastor Tom and Ginger had their youngest daughter in a Christian school.

"You have your child in a Christian school, but we can't put ours in one. We can't afford it."

The statement bothered the pastor enough that he began to pray about a Christian school his people could afford. The old dream of a school, birthed years before, had stayed with him. The newly acquired associate pastor Dick Bailey had a degree in education, and so did his wife, Marcia. Pastor Tom thought that, possibly, they would be the Lord's choice to start a Christian school.

In the meantime, other things were occupying his mind. The El Ada Storehouse was made available to the Community Christian Center for use as a food bank. The old barracks church, after serving as a youth center for a time, had been sold to the Senior Citizens for a dollar and moved to the Senior Citizen's site. A trench had been dug for water to irrigate the playground. The Billy Graham Crusade was in town. A number of the congregation were singing in the crusade choir and serving as counselors.

Months passed, and one night, Ginger had a vivid dream. In her dream, she was caring for several children. There was a violent storm outside. She could see things flying by the window. The building shook. The trees outside bent double. In the middle of the floor, five whirlwinds rose.

Ginger gathered the children into a corner. They were all terrified. Abruptly, an authoritative voice spoke aloud, "Feed the children! It's all right. Feed the children!" Ginger awoke with a start. The dream did not fade. It persisted daily.

Finally, she told Tom, "We need to see about getting our school started. I believe the dream was a directive from the Lord."

They visited some of the area schools and made inquiries. The Don Browns, former members of the Christian Center who had moved to Garden Valley, told them of their school at the Crouch Church. Pastor Tom and Ginger decided to visit that school.

They found the curriculum, Accelerated Christian Education, allowed students of different grade levels to all be in the same classroom. The curriculum was individualized so that each student learned at his own pace. The emphasis was not on how much was taught but on how the student learned. The curriculum was administered in bite-sized pieces, and the students each progressed at their own rate of speed. The church in Crouch was very pleased with the progress of its students. Only two teachers were hired. The desks were handmade by the congregation, and the curriculum was ordered as needed. Thus, the cost to the church was minimal.

By July 1983, the Baileys had moved on. Nevertheless, Pastor Tom took the idea back to his church board, and they decided to send him and Ginger to the Texas Headquarters of Accelerated Christian Education for training. After a period of intensive instruction, they returned to Garden City, ready to go to work.

Desks were purchased from Central Assembly Church, which had formerly housed such a school. Two teachers—Jerry and Barbara Grimm, members of the congregation—were hired. Volunteer monitors—Sue Palmer, Vickie Harwood, and Beth Campbell, also congregational members—were secured. Ginger, whose college degree was in secondary education, was the volunteer principal. She set about interviewing parents and students for enrollment.

Some members of the congregation, who did not want a school, left the church. There were five of these families. The rest of the congregation gave their prayer support to the school.

Tithing members of the Christian Center were not required to pay tuition. Non-tithing parents were required to pay the cost of the curriculum for their children.

The school staff had an intensive professional training period.

When the time came to order curriculum for the first time, the staff had very little understanding of what would be needed. They gathered early one morning to begin their work. A young woman appeared in the office doorway, saying she would help with the ordering. She reported that she had experience with the curriculum. The staff had not seen her before or has seen her since. She simply appeared, helped with the order, and left. Those present did not even remember her name. They believed she had been sent from God.

By September 27, 1983, eighteen students had been enrolled, of whom all were children or grandchildren of the congregational members. School was conducted during the weekdays. In the evenings and on the weekend, the desks were folded up and pushed back so the church could use the facility. In the mornings, the students and teachers put the school back together—a process that took about ten minutes. For the next sixteen years, the Community Christian Center operated the school known as the Community Christian Learning Center. The largest enrollment, after the educational building was completed, was sixty-two students. The smallest enrollment was the first year. Over twenty-five students graduated from the school, and by 1998, some second-generation children were enrolled. The Lord blessed and provided for this work.

Chapter 30

The Lord's Supply

Three years after beginning the Christian school in the church building, the school was "bursting its seams." There were kindergarten classes and elementary classes on one side of the sanctuary. Junior-high and high-school classes were held in the fellowship hall. There was a class meeting in the library. It was necessary to formulate plans for a larger multipurpose building equipped with classrooms and a gym. As yet, the neighborhood children had no place to meet and play after school when the weather was bad.

Once more, the congregation brought the need before the Lord. It would be an impossible task without his help. The Lord had already started to answer before they brought the need before him. Mrs. Forrey, a longtime friend of the Christian Center, had written the Community Christian Center into her will. When she passed away, she left $25,000 to the center, along with some property she owned on Capital Boulevard. On that property, there was the Jackson's Texaco Station. For several years, the center received money from that lease until they sold the property. The money they realized from the sale went a long way toward the building of a new multipurpose building.

Meanwhile, some exciting events were taking place in the church building. An unexpected visit from a concerned Christian resulted in a new avenue of ministry opening. Plans were being made to expand the walk-in cooler to include a large freezer. Lee Watson, who had accepted the Lord at the Christian Center some years before, was put in charge of the food bank. He had prior training in the food industry, so he was able to do an exceptional job. Lee also helped as an administrator of the building and grounds. He was gifted with many talents that enhanced the ministry of the center.

A new associate minister, Brad Bradburn, was hired to help the pastor with the workload.

The congregation continued to look for needs, pray about them, and try to meet them. As new areas of ministry opened up, the Lord supplied those who could help with the work

Chapter 31

A Time of Testing

In 1987, the congregation enthusiastically broke ground for the new multipurpose building. This was to be a work of faith, but none knew at the time how severe the testing would be.

The multipurpose building was to be built directly behind the church building, with the roof of each connected. As the footings were set up, many volunteers were ready to help with the task. Work on the building progressed, and by August 1988, they began to pour the concrete for the floor of the multipurpose building. The Lord provided for the plumbing fixtures, and the underground plumbing was in place before the floor was poured. The first cinder block was placed, and the walls began to rise. After two stories of cinderblock were in place, limited framing began. The restrooms, shower rooms, and partitions between the office and the gym were framed. The volunteer crew worked hard.

Then the time of testing came. One day, the crew was working on the walls, and the next day, the work had ceased. Money had stopped flowing in. The building stood stark against the sky, walls rising two stories up, but the work had stopped. There were a few partitions but no roof. There were no windows. The twenty-eight-thousand-square-foot building, which had been the dream of the Community Christian Center, appeared to have become a nightmare.

Each time the wind blew hard, the congregation prayed the walls wouldn't fall down. Friends of Pastor Tom shook their heads in disbelief. "Didn't you have a plan for its completion?" seemed to be the unspoken question.

Satan himself often reminded Pastor Tom, "What man of you will start a building and not count the cost lest it remains unfinished? And folks will go by and wag their heads, saying, 'Thou fool!'"

Every morning, when Pastor Tom went to work, it seemed that a banner hung around the building, emblazoned with the words "Thou fool!"

Wanting to keep the dream alive, Ginger scheduled the school's year-end banquet to be held out in the "new school building." Pastor Tom scheduled a fund-raising auction out there, but their efforts seemed to no avail. Some members of the congregation became discouraged and even critical. It seemed Satan would chuckle with glee.

Four years of testing went by. The dream still lived in Pastor Tom's heart, but it was a vibrant reality in God's mind.

The outside of the unfinished new school building.

Inside the entryway in the unfinished new school building.

Chapter 32

Revival of a Dream

Time and again, God strode into the affairs of men and placed an individual who was able to accomplish his purposes. In the case of the uncompleted building, he placed Glenn Lungren on the grounds at Community Christian Center for a meeting that was unrelated to the programs of the church. Glenn was there for a meeting to support a mayoral candidate for Garden City.

What he saw at the Community Christian Center bothered him. He couldn't get it out of his mind. The exterior walls were up. Still, there was no roof. There were no windows. The plastic plumbing was beginning to crumble.

Glenn was a retired vice-president of marketing for West One Bank. Getting money for worthwhile projects was his specialty. He had raised money to put a cross on Table Rock. He helped raise money to launch the first musical production as part of Boise's Music Week in 1959. He was the person who directed the fund-raising for the Senior Citizen Center in Meridian. He was knowledgeable, energetic, and enthusiastic about how to raise funds for this project as well. The Lord continued to prod Glenn's mind about the need for a school and gym for the Garden City children.

One morning, he appeared in Pastor Tom's office with a request. "Will you let me help you raise the money to complete the building?" he demanded.

"Give me about two seconds to reply to that!" exclaimed Pastor Tom.

"I was surprised but *not* surprised," Tom reflected on the conversation. "That's the way things work around here. People show up when there are needs. It's fun if you enjoy that sort of thing and if you have a strong heart."

Glenn Lungren had the contact with people the congregation didn't have. Much of the support came from people who knew him and had worked with him on other fund-raising projects.

One of the contributors was the Laura Moore Cunningham Foundation, a philanthropic organization started by a Boise family, which gave $250,000 over a three-year period.

"I was struck dumb by the progress they made with nothing," Joan Carley, the foundation's secretary-treasurer said. "They've done it with faith in God and whatever happened to come their way. They have moved mountains" (*Idaho Statesman*, March 1997).

But the congregation knew that they weren't the ones who moved the mountains. They served a mighty God.

Chapter 33

Celebration

In 1997, the school building had been completed. That year, the school had sixty-two students. It was also the year the congregation celebrated fifty years of the Community Christian Center's ministry in Garden City. They decided to make it a combined dedication of the new multipurpose building and the fiftieth-anniversary celebration. Plans were made to invite all former board members and Christian Center members and friends, construction workers and subcontractors, fund-raisers, and supporters to a celebration. The historians searched for old pictures and newspaper articles. A dinner was planned, and invitations were sent out.

The celebration of the completion of a miracle was held in the new gymnasium. The multipurpose building had been completed debt free and was to be dedicated to the glory of God. There were classrooms, a weight room, offices, and a nursery. The gymnasium included dressing rooms and restrooms. There was also a large stage, so programs and plays could be performed, with storage underneath for tables and chairs. In addition, there were storage shelves, a furnace room, a laundry room, and a toolroom. The gymnasium floor had a specially designed carpet rather than a wood floor. It had court lines for basketball, volleyball, and four-square games already woven in so the children wouldn't have to have special basketball shoes to come in and play. Pastor Tom envisioned many uses for the gymnasium, including flea markets, political rallies, bicycle rodeos, talent shows, and concerts.

The gym walls were decorated for the celebration with scores of bulletin boards, featuring pictures, newspaper articles, old church bulletins, and memorabilia.

Unknown to Pastor Tom and Ginger, family and friends had also planned the celebration as a tribute to their faithful ministry for the past thirty-eight years.

The whole event was an emotionally charged highlight of the Christian Center's fifty years of existence and a fitting tribute to God's faithfulness throughout the year

Chapter 34

The Women Who Supported the Ministry

It would be impossible to list all the supporters of the Community Christian Center. The Lord touched the hearts of so many. Many of the supporters were women who supported the ministry, much like the women in the Bible supported the Lord's ministry. Beginning with Mrs. Leisher, the center's founder; and continuing through Margaret Cobb Ailshie, Laura Moore Cunningham, Hazel Forney, Mildred McGrath, Mrs. Shaw and the ladies of the Nampa First Baptist Church, Sister Stephanie, Esther Davis; and on through Velma Morrison; and other names too numerous to mention, women played a significant role in the history. Listed below are a few examples of the women who helped:

The recreation program of the center was stalled because the plumbing was not completed. Taylor Robertson, an executive-board member, contacted Mrs. Ailshie and asked her to provide the money to finish paying for the completion of the plumbing. She did, and the recreation program went forward.

Hazel Forney was called upon whenever a need arose that the center couldn't meet without her help. Such projects included everything from clothing for the needy children to a roof for the church building. The piano in the sanctuary was one of her gifts. At her death, the center received the deed to the Texaco Service Station. That business was later sold, and the money was used to help build the school building.

Mildred McGrath furnished dinners for the executive-board meetings for many years.

Mrs. Shaw and the ladies from the First Baptist Church in Nampa, Idaho, spent hours sewing new clothing for the needy children.

Esther Davis furnished blankets, food, and clothing for the needs of the Christian Center. Later, she furnished money for the ongoing needs of the school.

Sister Stephanie began the soup kitchen at the center.

The Laura Moore Cunningham Foundation provided three hundred and fifty thousand dollars, in three installments, for the building of the school.

Velma Morrison added $ 50,000. She came down to the center and asked Pastor Tom if she could enjoy a meal at the soup kitchen. She introduced herself at the table as Velma and visited with the people who were eating there as if she were one of them. Later, she produced the gift for the school building.

Gladys Cole, one of our members, started the Garden City Library at the Christian Center. The women from the First Baptist Church's Ginger Blackburn Circle came and varnished the kitchen cabinets, stocked the pantry, and provided school supplies for many years for the school children. They also provided encouragement and ongoing prayer support for the Blackburns. Women's groups from churches all over Southern and Central Idaho provided regularly for the food pantry. Ruth Grothaus, one of our own members, served as a nurse at the health clinic during the years we operated it in our building. Many women served as Sunday-school teachers over the years.

We cannot leave this chapter without mentioning that the dynamic person behind the whole project of the Community Christian Center, the one who obeyed the voice of the Lord and established the center at his leading, was Mrs. Estle Leisher.

Chapter 35

But God

If either Mrs. Leisher or Pastor Tom had listened to men during the years from 1947 to 1997, God's will for Garden City would never have materialized the way it did. As the Scripture says, "Man may make his plans, but the final outcome is in God's hands" (Prov. 16:9).

Compare man's ideas with the Lord's in the following paragraphs:

The Baptists told Mrs. Leisher that establishing a Christian Center couldn't be done in 1947 because it would never be self-supporting. But God knew it would be.

One board member questioned the building of a playground, "Who knows what will be here in twenty years?" The year was 1961. But God knew.

The dean of Berkeley Baptist Divinity School told Tom, "Since you did not pass both sections of the comprehensive exam at the same time and since I feel the school has contributed all it can to your education, I will not be able to allow you to continue at the seminary, and since we do not feel you have the qualities necessary to become a successful pastor, we have decided to recommend to you that you leave school and get yourself a job as a youth minister since that seems to be the only aptitude you have. Because you can only do that successfully for about ten years, you should make plans for what you want to do for the rest of your life after ten years as a youth minister." But God had other ideas.

One couple said, "We will never finish this project [the multipurpose building], and we are not going to stay around to see it fail." So they left. But God did not.

In 1964, the CEO of a Boise foundation pledged $5,000 in matching funds since $10,000 would build a building for any program in Garden City. However, when the congregation of the Center presented the chairman of the board a check for $5,000 to match that pledge, he changed his mind. His decision, however, was worth much more than $5,000 to motivate the congregation to renewed commitment to prayer and hard work to make sure that this project was completed. But God knew that this would be a turning point.

In 1965, a Garden City resident (regarding building the new church structure) said, "Building materials are too expensive now. Wait until the prices come down." The prices did not come down, but God supplied.

In October 1965, another board member said, "The money in the building fund is a trust and cannot be used to raise additional funds for the building." But God knew what to do.

Harold Ellis, when approached to be superintendent of the building project for the new church in 1969, said, "I can't do this job. Can't you see that I've lost a leg?" But God knew that he could use his good mind.

After Tom talked to the ministers in Clearfield, Utah, about the construction of a new church building, a fellow pastor questioned him, "You say that time after time you went to the mailbox and found the exact amount of money that was needed to keep the building going. What would you have done if there had not been a check in the mailbox? That was really foolish." But God didn't call it foolishness. He called it faith.

In 1991-1995, during the unexplained four-year pause in construction of the multipurpose building, the congregation's faith was severely tested. Satan plastered the building with a big sign that read, "What man building a building does not first sit down and count the cost lest when it is half finished, he is unable to complete it? And the world, passing by, shakes it head, saying, 'You fool!'" But God had his own plan in mind.

The Community Christian Center stands as a tribute to what the Lord can do through women and men who rely on Him wholly in faith.

Countless individuals have contributed time, money, energy, and prayers to its work. The ministry has touched thousands of lives.

Back in 1947, no one knew what would become of the ministry of the Community Christian Center. Its humble beginnings lent no hint of the outreach that would result and the lives that would be changed. But God knew.